# HARLEY-DAVIDSON
## *THE MOTORCYCLE THAT BUILT A LEGEND*

*Photography by Gerald Foster*

**Motorbooks International**
Publishers & Wholesalers Inc.

First published in 1986 by Motorbooks International
Publishers & Wholesalers Inc, PO Box 2, 729 Prospect
Avenue, Osceola, WI 54020 USA

© Gerald Foster, 1986

Motorbooks International is a certified trademark, registered
with the United States Patent Office

Printed and bound in Hong Kong

The information in this book is true and complete to the best
of our knowledge. All recommendations are made without
any guarantee on the part of the author or publisher, who also
disclaim any liability incurred in connection with the use of
this data or specific details

**Library of Congress Cataloging-in-Publication Data**
Foster, Gerald.
  Harley-Davidson: the motorcycle that built a legend.
  1. Harley-Davidson motorcycle. I. Title.
TL448.H3F68 1986 629.2'275 86-12772 ISBN 0-87938-220-1

Motorbooks International books are also available at
discounts in bulk quantity for industrial or sales-promotion
use. For details write to Special Sales Manager at the
Publisher's address

We recognize that Sportster, Electra-Glide, Super Glide, Duo
Glide, Harley-Davidson, H-D, Low Rider, Wide Glide, Tour Pak,
Fat Bob, Roadster, Softail and any other Harley names,
including the one word Harley itself, and emblems or
designations in this book are the property of the Harley-
Davidson Motor Company, Inc. And we gratefully use them
with permission. This is not an official publication of the
Harley-Davidson Motor Company, Inc.

**Cover photography:** Rolling thunder! Both on the blacktop and in the
heavens, there's nothing better than riding a Harley. Bike's a Softail (from
here), with belt rear drive and the V2 engine, designed to recapture solid rear
end of the custom chopper; suspension's underneath.

**Page 1:** H-D and the Statue of Liberty; America's finest plays its part in saving
America's welcoming lady. For 1986 the closest there was to a special edition
was the Liberty Edition paint and graphics for the FXRT model.

**Title page:** Milwaukee goes to Daytona. Bike Week is big for H-D. This semi
hauls display bikes for all to see. Daytona is for Harley-Davidson what America
is for apple pie.

**Right:** Mid-fifties Panhead Duo-Glide proves that Harleys simply go on
forever (with some tender loving care).

# Contents

# Introduction

I am sometimes asked to explain the mystique of the Harley-Davidson motorcycle. On such occasions I usually look as though I'm giving the question a lot of thought before I finally admit to not really having an answer. I don't think anyone else does either. There are the more conventional answers, of course, which usually revolve around patriotism by virtue of the machine being made in the USA, and the type of image — good or bad — that having a Harley can project.

There is also a view which holds that technological progress ain't necessarily for the best. I tend to lean toward this view, at least where motorcycles are concerned. Is it possible that Harleys are popular because they remind us of a much simpler time? A time when the Environmental Protection Agency, unleaded gasoline, electronic ignition, exhaust emission control and so on did not exist, and anyone with a lick of sense could fix a motorcycle beneath a shade tree in the front yard.

Of one thing, however, I am sure. A Harley-Davidson does have **style.** And no one in my opinion has ever put it better than author David Wright: "You don't just show up on a Harley. You **arrive.**"

Gerald Foster
Burbank, California

Because of time constraints in preparing this book it was necessary to call upon friends to help out with the photography. They are:

**PETE CHIODO** for **SOMETHING DIFFERENT.**
**MIL BLAIR, BUZZ BUZZELLI** and the **HARLEY-DAVIDSON MOTOR CO. INC.,** for **'LINERS.**
**BILL HOECKER** for the **1948 WR** in **RESTORATION.**

Thank you all.

It is impossible to put together a book like this one without a lot of help from other people. And, as I have always managed to forget to include the name of at least one person in previous books, I decided a more generic "thank you" might work better this time. You all know who you are, of course, so here goes. Without all of you this book would still be a pile of photographs sitting on a desk somewhere. I thank you that it isn't.

**Right**
There are probably more custom Harleys than stock ones. Designer/builders Mil Blair and Paul Larquier went for the utmost simplicity with this 91 cu. in. creation. Clean is neat.

6

# **1 STEAMER**

Millions of people the world over are fascinated by steam-powered vehicles but few have felt the need to produce their very own Harley steamer. Leonard J. Washburn, a radiator repairman from Rubidoux, California, did, however, in 1939.

Having previously owned a 1918 Stanley Steamer automobile, Washburn constructed the machine, apparently after having been talked out of buying another steam-powered two-wheeler that was for sale in San Francisco. According to a late-fifties article in an issue of **Mechanix Illustrated** magazine, the 74 Harley engine was replaced with a Toledo steam engine from a 1902 automobile. Total time and cost for the conversion was 14 months and $650.

Having bought the Harley steamer at an estate sale, Louie Peterson, owner of the A&A Motorcycle Museum in Arcadia, California, is currently in the process of refurbishing the machine and putting it back into operating condition.

A locomotive sight glass shows the level of water in the saddle tanks at the rear of the Flyer.

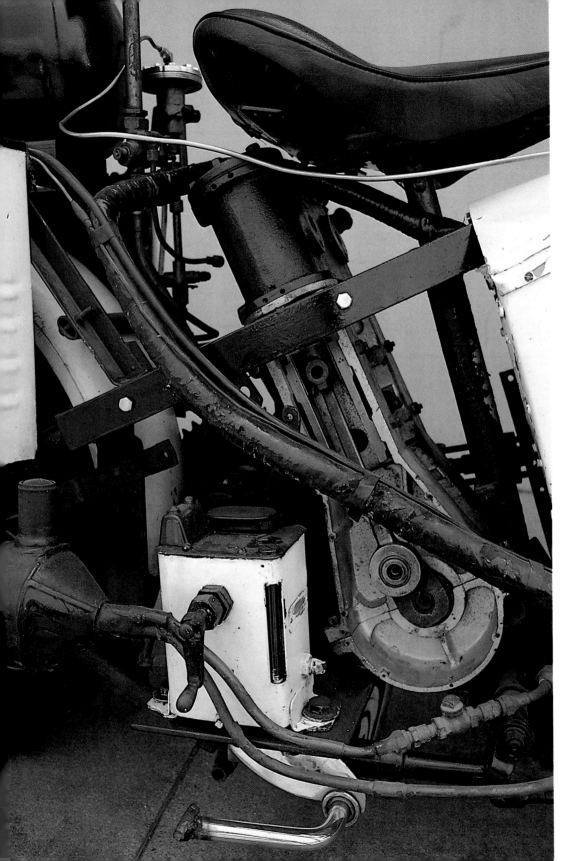

The tube resembling a muffler is a condenser, a device for reducing the exhausted steam back to water. Butane to fire the boiler is carried in the tank behind the rider. The black object immediately behind the butane tank is a battery needed for lights.

The cylinders are lubricated from a pump to the left of the crankshaft.

The Toledo steam engine, vintage 1902. The foot-operated throttle allows steam to enter the cylinders where it expands to force down the pistons and transmit power to the rear wheel by chain. No clutch or gearbox is required.

The brass whistle was the first and simplest part to refurbish. Controls give the impression of being the result of Washburn's worst nightmare.

According to an article in a late-fifties issue of **Mechanix Illustrated**, performance of the 850 lb machine with a full head of steam was in excess of 100 mph. Water consumption was around 30 mpg while butane averaged 35 mpg.

**Following pages**
All of the previous photographs were taken prior to restoration; the accompanying photograph shows Louie Peterson's Harley-Davidson steamer as it appears today, totally restored and in fully operating condition.

# 2 WALL ART

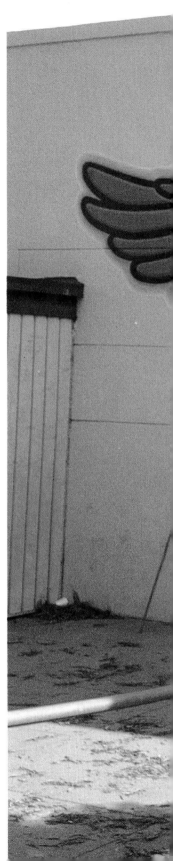

A campus is not one of the more usual places you might expect to find a 16-by-30-foot Harley-Davidson mural, but Pasadena City College, California, boasts one enthusiast's tribute to the marque. The work of Dennis Eagleson, a student of the sign arts program, the mural was inspired by many others of varying subjects which began appearing all over Los Angeles prior to the 1984 Olympics.

# MOTOR
## HARLEY-DAVIDSON
## CYCLES

DEDICATED TO MY DAUGHTER,
VALERIE LENISE EAGLESON
AND TO ALL THE RIDERS OF THE
WIND, PAST AND PRESENT...
RESPECTFULLY,
DENNIS JAMES EAGLESON
—— MARCH 20th 1997 ——

On busy Laurel Canyon in an industrial area of North Hollywood, California, this drag racing Shovelhead mural must appear like freedom and light to the many thousands of commuters who pass by it every day. (Only on a Sunday, without the parked cars and the continuous stream of traffic, is it possible to photograph the complete mural.) The brushwork of Dennis Olsen, the mural stands proud on the wall of P&B Balancing, a business catering to Harley drag racers.

Preceding page
Boot Hill Saloon is **the** watering hole during Bike Week.

The production and sale of Harley beer for specific events such as Daytona or Sturgis has proven to be a marketing coup, since demand usually outstrips supply. Additionally the cans have become collector items, especially since event and date have been added to the artwork.

Following pages
Daytona aerial billboard.

DRINK HARLEY BEER

A somewhat unusual and practical alternative to finding accommodation during Speed Week. Peterbilt hauls Low Rider.

**Following pages**
The beach at Daytona is one of the very few in the US on which vehicles are allowed, and parkin' and cruisin' are the order of the day.

The rat bike as a serious art form demands attention. Smitty, owner of this gem, is happy if one item added per year enhances the overall look of his Knucklehead.

Following pages
In a modern version of **Gone with the Wind,** would Rhett Butler ride a Harley? Bike looks like a highly modified Super Glide.

Much of the Daytona traffic is stop and go during Bike Week, but with so many bikes to check out and pretty girls to look at no one seems to mind the delays.

Pretty girls and Harleys can be spotted throughout Daytona during Bike Week. Linda Wilson attracted a lot of attention.

The annual Rat's Hole custom show on the boardwalk attracts entrants from all over the US and thousands of interested enthusiasts who appreciate bikes as mobile works of art.

And the winner in the
Dresser class is...

Stylish Shovel.

This restored near-fifty-year-old side-valver looks better (and different) than when it left the factory.

Love this chopper down
by the beach.

Whether you love or hate murals, they do warrant some attention.

Okay, okay, so it's not quite your style.

SHELLS
BEACHWEAR
T-SHIRTS
SOUVENIRS
JEWELRY
PARKING

GIFTS BEACH

Hog Heaven BAR-B-Q

OPEN

CUSTOMER PARKING

*Goddam right!*

# 4 YORK, PA

While Milwaukee is still home to Harley-Davidson, final assembly takes place 800 miles away in York, Pennsylvania. Idle in 1982, when Harley-Davidson was owned by the conglomerate AMF, the former bowling and defense plant was put into operation at a time when the company was producing 50,000 motorcycles a year, and had literally run out of manufacturing space in Milwaukee.

**Following pages**
Evolution V2 engines and transmissions still manufactured in Milwaukee are shipped to York for final assembly.

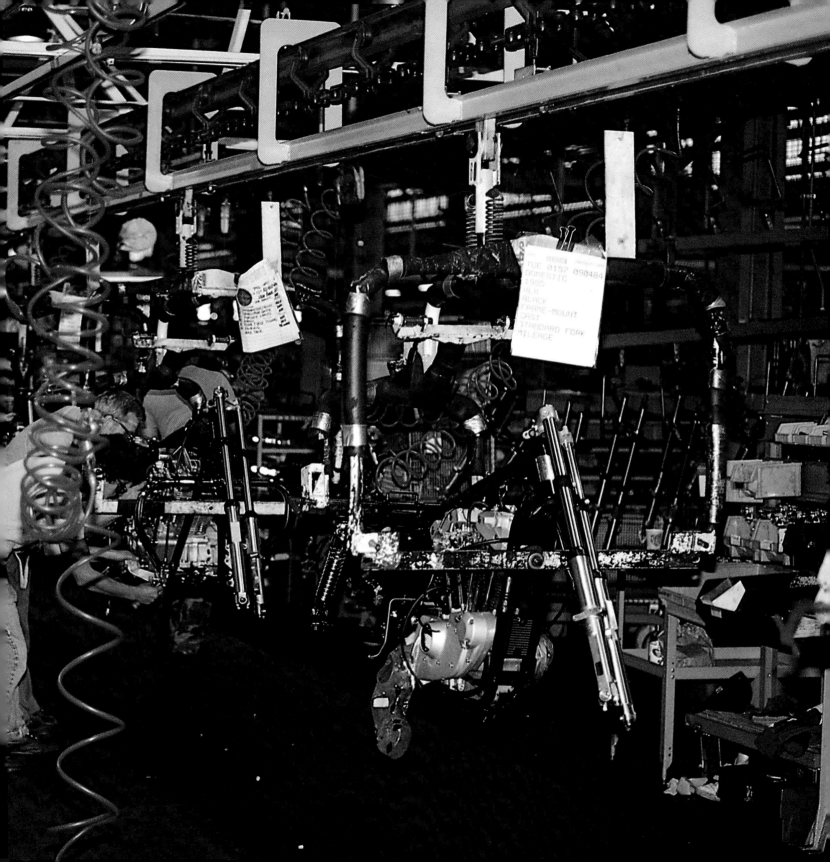

Employees exhibit a pride in workmanship and love of product not usually found in "ordinary" manufacturing plants.

**Following pages**
A ticket, which accompanies each motorcycle along the production line, and a computerized parts delivery system, which delivers the correct model parts in the required colors, ensure that machines are built according to the production schedule. Production schedules are prepared from information supplied by the sales department.

**Preceding pages**

At the end of the production line each motorcycle is started and put through a series of engine and transmission tests to ensure performance is within specifications.

Prior to shipment the motorcycles are partially dismantled and crated.

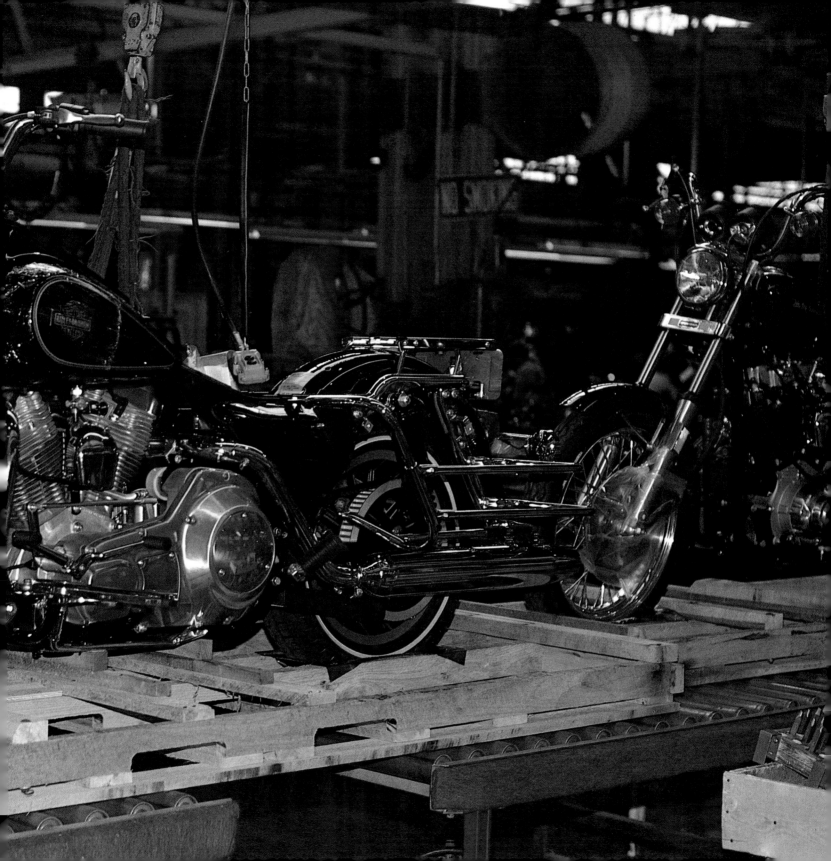

# 5 BODY ADORNMENTS

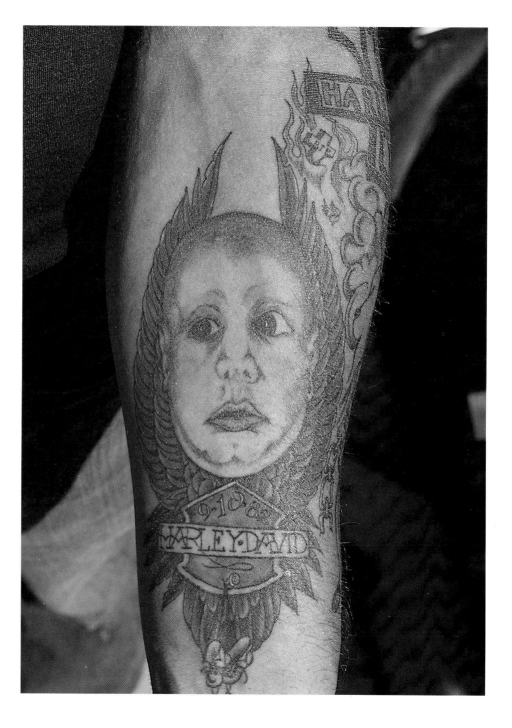

Proud of his new son, who is named Harley David, Daniel Lloyd of Maryland had the boy's likeness tattooed on his arm.

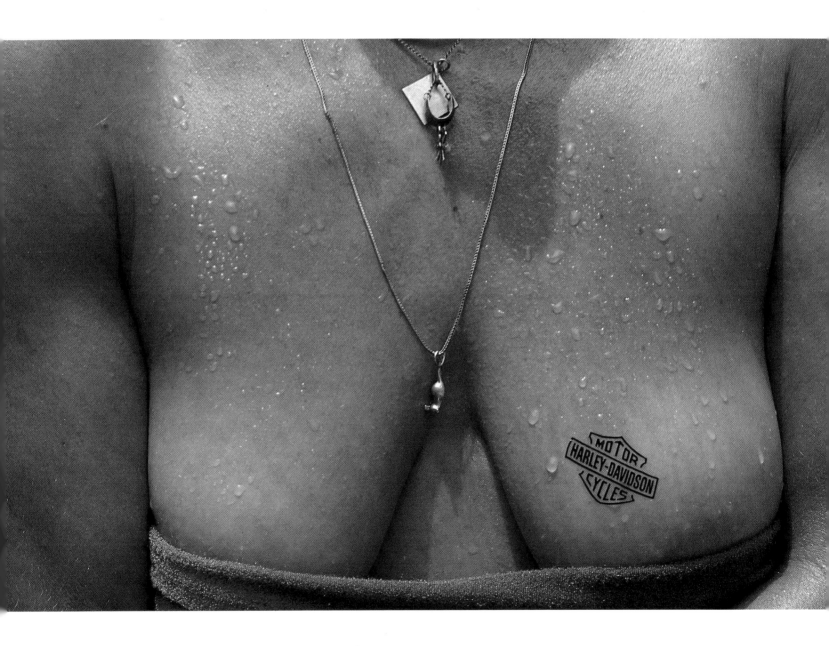

Stick-on tattoos are for those whose commitment is not one hundred percent.

Check out the detail on this Harley-Davidson.

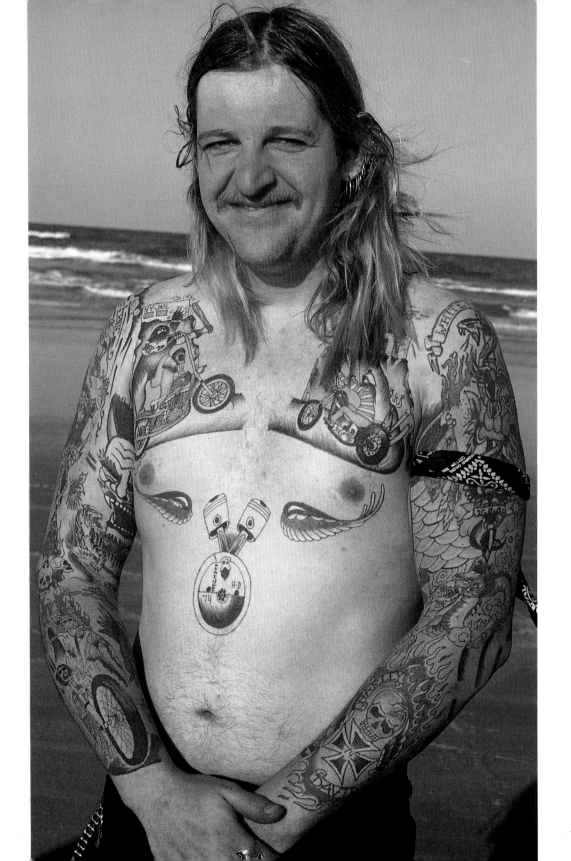

# 6 RESTORATION

A nattily attired Bill Hoecker aboard his restored 1931 DLD side-valve Special Sports Solo.

**Following pages**
An immaculately restored 1931 DLD side-valve Special Sports Solo. Making its debut in 1929 the 45 cu. in. model became an instant hit and remained in production in two-wheel machines until 1951, and three-wheel Servi-Car models for a further 22 years.

A 1948 WR with factory-manufactured lightweight frame. The W series side-valve engine dominated US racing until production ended in 1951.

No one is quite sure how many restorations were completed by Bud Ekins in this steel building located in North Hollywood, California, but a conservative figure is two hundred plus. Bud has since moved to larger quarters, which he is currently in the process of "customizing."

# 7
# MARRIAGE

Bride and groom getting married and riding away on the groom's Harley-Davidson is not unusual. The bride riding away on her own custom Sportster is, however, a little more unusual.

# 8 MILITARY

The machine is complete, down to dummy hand grenades, ammunition and original military-issue canned food.

Having studied the subject for some years, John T. McKenna of Fayetteville, New York, knows Harley-Davidson's World War II military model, the WLA, inside and out. In addition to being a leading authority on the model, John is also a man who enjoys nothing more than taking his WLA to Daytona where, in his authentic uniform, he entertains hundreds of interested bikers with information and stories about the motorcycle many consider among the greatest ever built.

The steel rod attached to the handlebars was protection against decapitation, since it wasn't unusual for the enemy to stretch a steel cable (which the rider would not see until it was too late) between two trees across country roads. Socks placed over mirrors prevented the sun from flashing on them and alerting the enemy to the rider's presence and location. If caught away from base for a night a WLA rider would utilize empty food cans and a coil of wire carried on the front fender to fashion a trip-wire alarm around his camp.

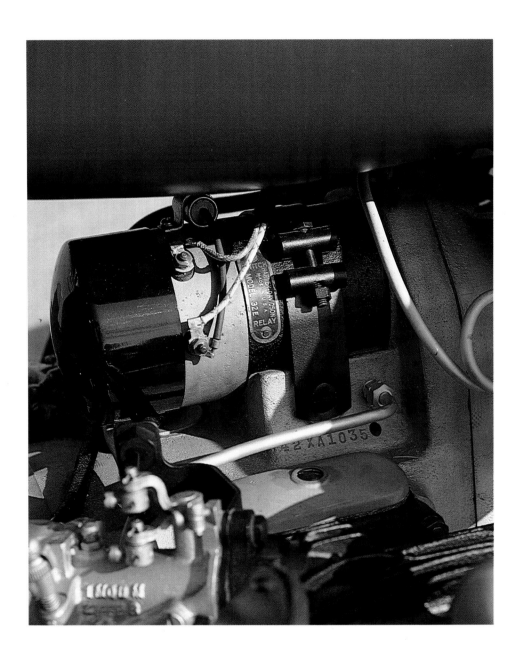

The XA was a copy of the BMW horizontally opposed 45 cu. in. twin-cylinder engine and shaft drive with metric dimensions converted to inches. Disc-wheel models were intended for service in the deserts of North Africa.

While the WLA was an incredibly successful motorcycle, the XA was not so lucky. At the request of the US Army, Harley-Davidson produced a copy of the BMW that the Germans used with great success in North Africa. The Army felt that the addition of the heavy-duty XA would round out its motorcycle transport. Unfortunately, the war in North Africa was won by the time the XA became operational, and the escalating war in the Pacific relied on the four-wheel-drive Jeep rather than the motorcycle. The XA was never produced in a civilian version after the war, and very few of the original one thousand ordered by the Army remain.

One of the few remaining rifle scabbards which have been located.

# 9 HILLCLIMB

In excess of 100 cu. in. the engine runs on a high percentage of nitro. The machine requires an extra-long swing arm to maintain stability on the extremely steep hills. The engine is fired by a hand-held starter that plugs into the end of the crankshaft and is powered from batteries on the cart. Fabricated guides help limit the derailing problems associated with the necessarily long drive chains.

In the world of fire-breathing exhibition class hillclimbers, #1 rated rider Kerry Peterson invariably wrestles this Harley-Davidson up and over the crest of some seemingly impossibly steep hills to take home the prize money.

**Following pages**
Kerry Peterson on his way to a winning run.

Steel paddles which attach to the rear tire are an absolute must for attacking the near impossible hills.

Following pages
Asked by a customer to build a Sportster with a different look gave Californian Bob Peysar, owner of San Fernando Motorcycle Service, an opportunity to build a machine incorporating many of his own ideas. The project began with Peysar mating a 1972 engine with an aftermarket frame and then spending many hours designing and fabricating new parts, and modifying other parts (including the frame), which now constitute the completed bike. Peysar's five-quart wraparound oil tank does much to improve the look of the machine.

Aftermarket dual-disc brakes provide stopping power at the front end.

Getting this FX-style rear wheel and the complete disc-brake mechanism to fit was a time-consuming task.

There are considerable numbers of pre-1975 Sportster engines in use which have the brake lever on the left, and the shift lever on the right. A lot of thought went into the design of the forward controls to get the shift lever to cross over to the left, and the brake lever to cross over to the right.

Discarding the Narrow Glide front end for being too narrow, and the Wide Glide front end for being too wide, Peysar decided to fabricate his own two-inch-wider-than-stock triple trees.

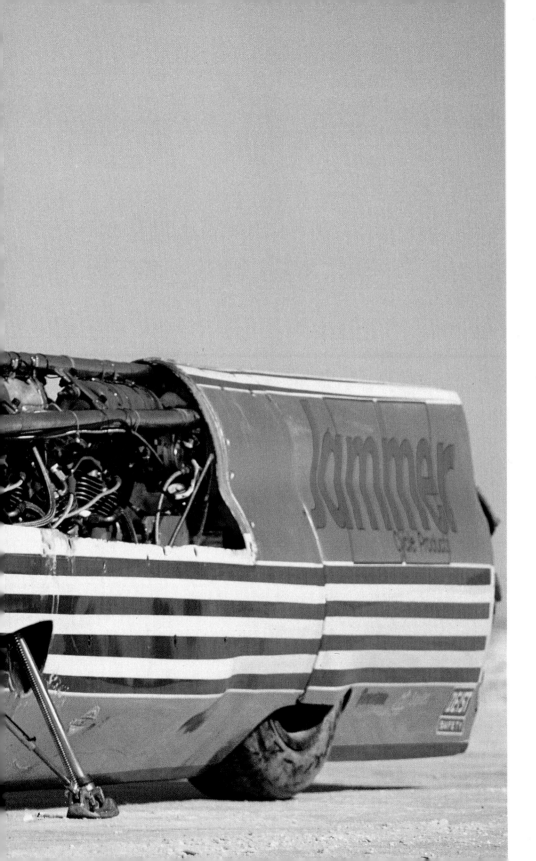

# 'LINERS

In the world of "go fast" motorcycles the ultimate ride has to be in a cigar-shaped tube into which one or two nitro-burning engines have been shoehorned. The place is the Bonneville Salt Flats in Utah, the object is a speed record. Going for a record is both hard work and time consuming. Additionally, out on the salt, a hundred miles from anywhere, Murphy's Law, which states that "anything that can go wrong will" comes into play, and usually with a vengeance. In the last ten years, two Harley-Davidson-powered Streamliners have had considerable success on the salt. They aren't the fastest two-wheeled machines on earth but in a world where increasing the number of cylinders and valves is the accepted route to more power and speed, the Harley-Davidson V-twin engine still manages to give a good account of itself.

Awaiting the right conditions. The Jammer Cycle Products 3000 cc twin-engined Harley Streamliner, driven by Dave Campos, ran an official 279.155 mph on the salt in 1978. A one-way run at 294 mph two years earlier could not be backed up by a second run in the opposite direction, because of transmission damage.

**Following pages**
**Tenacious**, designed and built by Denis Manning of San Jose, California, powered by a single 115 cu. in. Harley engine, ran an official 276.656 mph on Salt Flats in September 1985 with Dan Kinsey at the controls. Purposely undergeared to run on a shortened track, this speed is expected to be bettered in 1986, following a year of development and a full five miles of salt on which to run. **Tenacious** at speed.

# 12

## *RACER*

She is Tammy Kirk; a very fast and competent expert who, but for one slip when she momentarily got off the groove, almost made the National final at the May 1986 San Jose Mile.

The alloy XR-750 has been going since 1972, and is still going strong although in recent times the unmentionable threat from the Far East has materialized and these bulletproof rockets are no longer invincible. What a dirt-track Honda will never be, though, is immortalized as the very soul of H-D.

No two XRs are the same, as every one is modified in some way. Engine is an over-square 45 cu. in. 45-degree overhead valve vee twin blasting out 90 odd horsepower. When geared for the oval mile, 130-plus mph can be lit up, all with no front brake! Weight is around 320 lb. thus acceleration is electrifying.

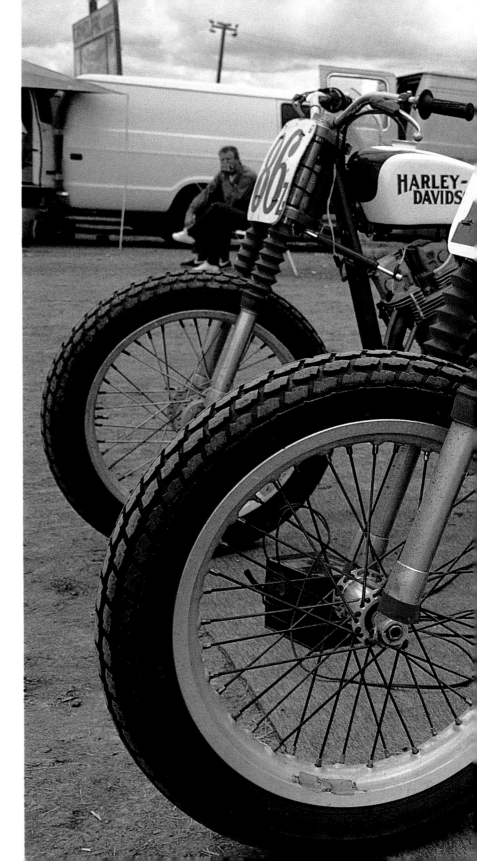

# SOMETHING DIFFERENT 13

Light in weight, low to the ground, street legal and good drag strip performance were the parameters set prior to building this 91 cu. in. 420 lb. Harley. In addition, it had to look good! Designed and built by Mil Blair and Paul Larquier, the machine attracts attention wherever it goes.

# DID YOU KNOW

In the late 1930s Dale Drake of Los Angeles began modifying Harley-Davidson Knucklehead engines for use in quarter-mile midget race cars. Known as a Drake, the engine featured water-cooled cylinders, dual carburetors and an increase in capacity from 61 to 90 cu. in. Usually mounted crosswise in the chassis enabled an in-or-out gearbox to be bolted directly to the crankshaft. There was no clutch. The ability to "hook up" coming out of turns made the Drake competitive with four-cylinder Offenhauser-powered cars on certain tracks, but a cooling system which used no pump could not handle the heat generated in longer races, or on longer tracks. In addition, vibration in the big engine was a problem; either the engine shook the car to pieces, or wore out the driver before the end of the race. The Drake engine had one other quirk: the seeming inability to run on both cylinders at low speeds such as warmup laps. The "pop, pop, popping" sound caused by the misfire, and the vibration problem, were, however, part of the magic of the Drake, according to those who remember them, and the reason the engines were affectionately referred to as shakers, and popsicles, or poppers.

One of the few remaining Drake engines which mounted lengthwise in the chassis utilized a chain to drive the rear wheels.

# A SAD STORY

"He wakes me up banging a .38 up and down on my breastbone. 'It's no good. I can't live without you, baby, so finish me off now,' he says, handing me the gun. Well, I was pissed I can tell ya 'cause here's this dumb husband, who I'd thrown out for good earlier, now breaking into my house and scaring the shit outa me by waving a loaded gun in my face. 'Finish me off, Baby. I'm nothing without you.' He was drunk and kept on repeating the same old line as he followed me to the closet from out of which I took my double-barreled twelve-gauge. 'Leroy,' I said, 'if you don't leave now I'm going to kill your f...... Harley.' But instead of listening to me, Leroy was trying to find enough words to put together for another of his 'Finish me off, baby,' sentences. As I was loading the shells, my mother — I guess she woke up from the commotion — appeared in the doorway. She had one of those 'I knew it would come to this' faces on her, which was made worse by her not having any teeth in. I told Leroy this was his last chance to leave, but he was more interested in trying to get Momma to get me to kill him. I don't think he realized what an ally she was to him at that moment. So, with both of them in tow I headed out to the garage where I knew Leroy's 74 would be parked. Momma seemed to like the idea of blowing up Leroy's bike even more than she did of having me finish him off, and began shouting encouragement. Leroy, on the other hand, too drunk to know what the f... was going on, stood there in a daze as I squeezed off what I thought was one, but was actually both barrels. Well, the force of both barrels going off together was enough to alter my aim some, kind of upwards..."

"...Instead of the engine, the shells hit the gas tank. How we all didn't get killed in the explosion, or the fire which burnt down the garage, I'll never know. Too bad about the bike too; no Harley deserves to die that way."